Examination of Conscience
for Little Ones

Written by Kimberly Fries

Copyright © 2019 Kimberly Fries. All rights reserved.

www.mylittlenazareth.com

No part of this book may be reproduced by any means without the written permission of the author.

First Edition: February 2019

Cover by Sue Kouma Johnson

ISBN-13: 9781795585811

*To remain a child before God
means to recognize our nothingness,
to expect everything from God.
It is not to become discouraged over our failings,
for children fall often, but they are too little
to hurt themselves very much.
- St. Therese*

Go in front of a crucifix or the Blessed Sacrament.

Kneel down or sit in front of Jesus and make the Sign of the Cross.

CALL UPON THE HOLY SPIRIT.

Come, Holy Spirit!

Help me to know my sins

and feel sorrow for them,

so that I may make a good confession.

First Commandment

I am the Lord your God. You shall not have strange gods before me.

Has God been the most
important person in my life?

Have I thought my toys, TV, or
sports are more important than God?

Have I taken time to
pray to God every day?

Second Commandment

You shall not take the name

of the Lord your God in vain.

Have I always spoken about God and Jesus with respect and reverence?

Have I used the name of God or Jesus in an angry or disrespectful way?

Have I treated holy things,
like rosaries or holy water,
with a lack of respect?

Third Commandment

Remember to keep holy the Lord's Day.

Do I prepare for Mass by praying before it starts?

Have I missed a Sunday Mass or complained about going to Mass?

Do I pay attention during Mass by praying the prayers and singing the songs?

Fourth Commandment

Honor your father and your mother.

Do I obey my parents by doing what they ask right away?

Have I been stubborn, moody, or pouty when my parents ask me to do my chores, homework, or help my brother or sister?

Have I disrespected my teachers or coaches with my actions?

Fifth Commandment

You shall not kill.

Have I been unkind or
unfair to others?

Do I share with others
and have patience?

Have I hurt someone by
yelling at them or hitting them?

Sixth Commandment

You shall not commit adultery.

Do I take care of my body
so I can be healthy and safe?

Do I respect my body
by dressing in a modest way?

Do I respect others
and give them privacy?

SEVENTH COMMANDMENT

You shall not steal.

Have I taken something
that does not belong to me?

Have I failed to return something
that I have borrowed?

Am I generous to my family and
friends with my time and belongings?

Eighth Commandment

You shall not bear false witness

against your neighbor.

Have I played unfairly or left anyone out when playing games?

Have I lied, cheated, or told just part of the truth?

Have I hurt someone by making up lies about him or her?

Ninth Commandment

You shall not covet your neighbor's wife.

Have I told or listened to dirty jokes or bad words?

Have I watched TV shows or movies that are not helping me learn how to be good?

Do I try to keep my mind on how to become a saint?

Tenth Commandment

You shall not covet your neighbor's goods.

Have I been jealous of the toys
and things my friends have?

Have I nagged my parents
about getting me more things?

Am I thankful for the many gifts
that God has given me?

Thank you, God, for helping me recognize my sins. Now I want to turn back to you and tell you that I am sorry in the Sacrament of Reconciliation. Please give me the grace to love you and my neighbor more perfectly.

O my God, I am heartily sorry for having offended Thee, and I detest all my sins because of Thy just punishments, but most of all because they offend Thee, my God, Who art all-good and deserving of all my love. I firmly resolve, with the help of Thy grace, to sin no more and to avoid the near occasions of sin.

Amen.

I love you Jesus!

I love you Mary!

Thank you for the gift of Reconciliation!

Make the
Sign of the Cross.

Collect All the My Little Nazareth Books

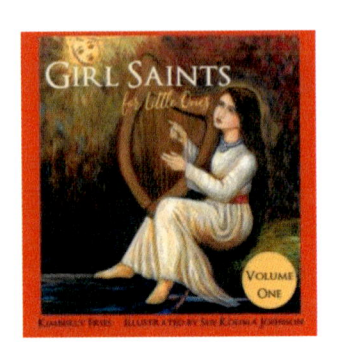

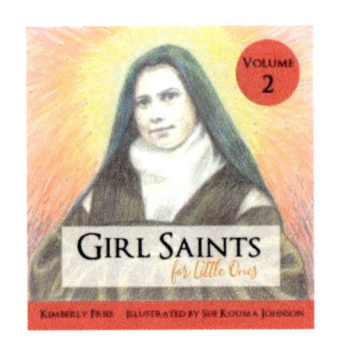

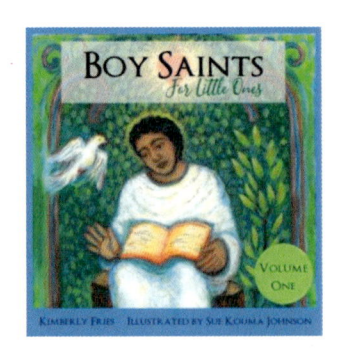

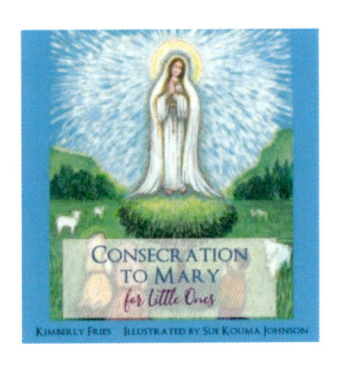

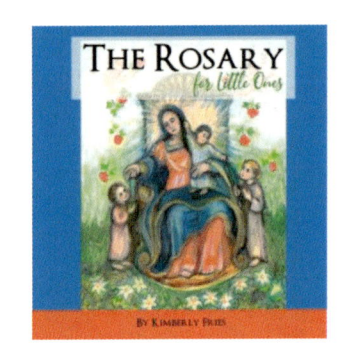

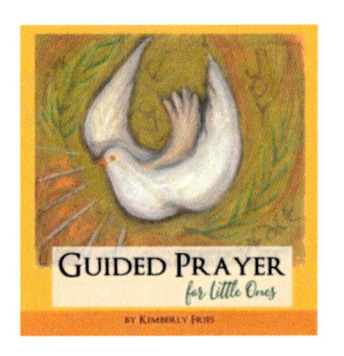

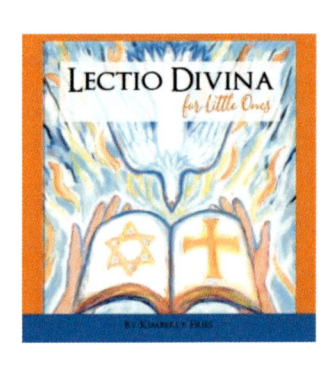

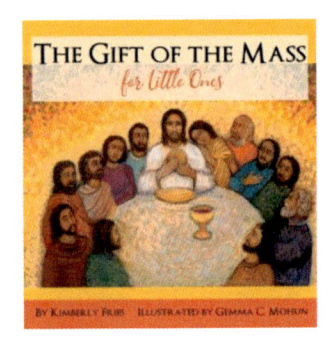

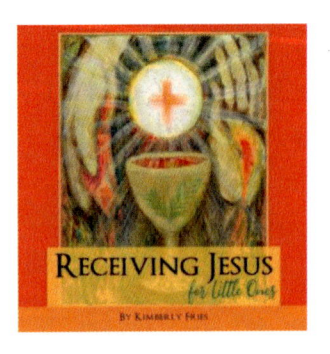

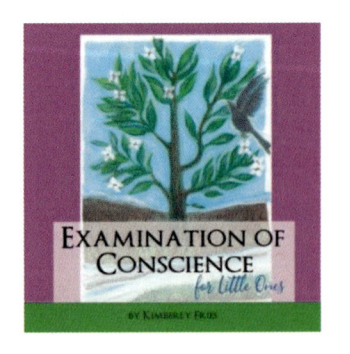

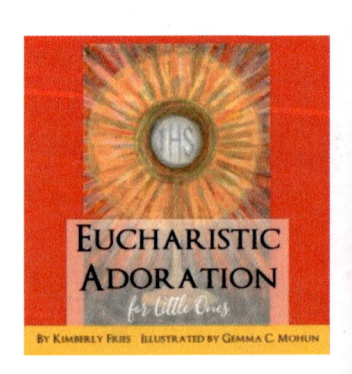

- Girl Saints for Little Ones, Volume One
- Girl Saints for Little Ones, Volume 2
- Boy Saints for Little Ones, Volume One
- Divine Mercy for Little Ones
- Consecration to Mary for Little Ones
- The Rosary for Little Ones
- Guided Prayer for Little Ones
- Lectio Divina for Little Ones
- The Gift of the Mass for Little Ones
- Receiving Jesus for Little Ones
- Examination of Conscience for Little Ones
- Eucharistic Adoration for Little Ones

Meet the Author

I'm Kimberly Fries, mom and Catholic author. I live in South Dakota with my husband and three children. Creating Catholic books to help children develop a personal relationship with God, Mary, and the saints has been such a joy for me. I pray that my books greatly bless your family and assist you in your journey to sanctity!

I would love to hear from you!

Please write a review at Amazon.com.

Want to be the first to know about my new releases?
Follow me on Facebook, Instagram, Youtube, and my blog!

Interested in getting wholesale, group, and parish prices?
E-mail me at mylittlenazareth@gmail.com

www.mylittlenazareth.com

Made in the USA
Las Vegas, NV
19 November 2020